# Jam Session

## Mia Hamm

**Terri Dougherty**

**ABDO Publishing Company**

# visit us at
# www.abdopub.com

Published by ABDO Publishing Company, 4940 Viking Drive, Suite 622, Edina, Minnesota 55435. Copyright © 2000 by Abdo Consulting Group, Inc. International copyrights reserved in all countries. No part of this book may be reproduced in any form without written permission from the publisher.

Printed in the United States.

Cover and Interior Photo credits:  AP Wide World Photos;  All-Sport Photos

Edited by Denis Dougherty

Sources:  Associated Press; Newsweek; New York Daily News; People Magazine; Sports Illustrated; Sports Illustrated For Kids; Time Magazine; ESPN Magazine; USA Today

## Library of Congress Cataloging-in-Publication Data

Dougherty, Terri.
    Mia Hamm / Terri Dougherty.
        p.   cm. -- (Jam Session)
    Includes index.
    Summary: A biography of one of the top female soccer players in the world, Mia Hamm, who helped the United States win a gold medal in soccer in the 1996 Olympics and the Women's World Cup in 1999.
      ISBN 1-57765-364-5 (hardcover)
      ISBN 1-57765-365-3 (paperback)
    1. Hamm, Mia, 1972-   --Juvenile literature.    2. Soccer players--United States--Biography--Juvenile literature. 3. Women soccer players--United States--Biography--Juvenile literature.
    [1. Hamm, Mia, 1972-  . 2. Soccer players. 3. Women--Biography.]   I. Title. II. Series.

GV942.7.H27 D68  2000
796.334'092--dc21
    [B]                                                                                        99-041950
                                                                                                    CIP
                                                                                                     AC

# Contents

# *Starting Off on the Right Foot*

Mia Hamm was in awe. A crowd of 78,972 fans was going crazy as the United States women's soccer team took on Denmark in the 1999 Women's World Cup. The American soccer team hadn't been used to this much attention. The crowd at Giants Stadium in East Rutherford, New Jersey, was the biggest ever to see a women's soccer game. Mia knew she and the team had to do well to keep soccer's red-hot popularity burning.

"When you get to a tournament like this, you want to start off on the right foot," Mia said. Mia was nervous, but she knew she couldn't let the crowd or the other team rattle her. Seventeen minutes after the game started, she took a pass from Brandi Chastain and slipped it past Denmark's goalie for the first goal of the game.

"When she gets the ball, you hold your breath," said Anson Dorrance, who coached Mia at the University of North Carolina.

In the seventy-third minute, Mia passed to Julie Foudy for the second goal of the game. Kristine Lilly scored later, and the U.S. won 3-0. "Mia was awesome," U.S. Coach Tony DiCicco said.

"She wanted the ball. She wanted the responsibility of feeding the players in the best area for a shot, or taking the shot herself."

When Mia zips down the soccer field with her ponytail flying and fires a ball with the speed of a missile, it's easy to see why she's called the best women's soccer player in the world. She quickly cuts through opposing defenses and is determined to score.

But Mia doesn't like being in the spotlight. She'd rather focus on her team, and how fun it is to get out and play. "Sports can do so much," she said. "It's given me a framework: meeting new people, confidence, self-esteem, time management, discipline, motivation. All these things I learned, whether I knew I was learning it or not, through sports."

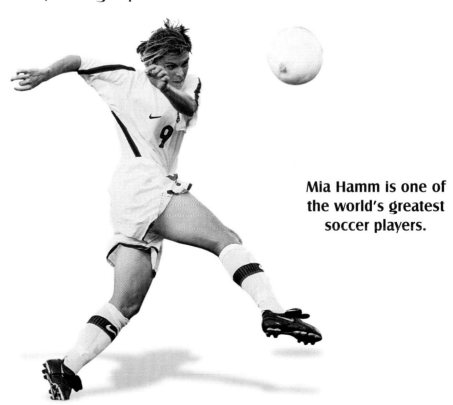

**Mia Hamm is one of the world's greatest soccer players.**

# Having a Ball

Mia was born in Selma, Alabama, on St. Patrick's Day in 1972, but she didn't live there long. Her father was in the Air Force and was soon transferred to Florence, Italy. Soccer is a very popular sport in Italy, and Mia saw her first game there. "I was two or three at the time," Mia said. "I remember my father taking us to games. We watched a lot of soccer."

Mia was too young to play, but that didn't keep her away from the soccer field. "My older brother and two older sisters played, and I watched them," Mia said. "I wanted to be like them, so I went to soccer practice and shagged balls for them. I couldn't compete in organized soccer until I was five."

Mia was too young for soccer, but she was old enough to dance. She took dance lessons at her mom's urging. Her mother was a ballerina, and Mia is named after one of her mother's former dance teachers.

Mia's mother wanted her to keep taking dance lessons. But when she was six, Mia left ballet class in tears. She wanted to play soccer instead. "At the beginning, I didn't like soccer more than other sports," Mia said. "I played so that I could be with my friends."

Soccer gave Mia something to count on as her family moved to five different places, following her dad's career. "While my mom and dad became very good at packing, I found stability on the soccer field," Mia said.

Mia also showed her athletic talent in baseball, basketball, and football. "I was in seventh grade, just one of the guys," Mia recalled. "I tried wide receiver. I kicked. I played quarterback once, but I wasn't very good at it. It was one of those things when you're young, you really don't think boy-girl. Who cares? They were my friends. They wanted me to play."

# Getting Her Kicks in One Sport

*A*nson Dorrance, the coach of the U.S. national women's soccer team, came to see Mia play when she was 14. Even though he didn't know what she looked like at first, he soon picked her out on the field.

The ball was kicked off and "this little girl took off like she was shot out of a cannon. I couldn't believe the athleticism," Dorrance recalled. Mia, however, downplays her talent. She says she doesn't remember doing that well in the game.

"I really struggled," she said, adding that she felt the college-age players she faced were much too good for her. Even though she was too modest to admit it, Mia's soccer talent was shining. She was living in Wichita Falls, Texas, and was a much better player than boys who were two or three years older.

At age 15, she became the youngest female ever to play for the U.S. women's soccer team. It wasn't easy. "Tactically, I didn't know what to do," she recalled. "During fitness sessions, I was dying. I would cry half the time."

But she didn't give up. She told herself she would never be out of shape again. Mia played her first game with the national team in China.  Six months later, Dorrance told her,  "Mia, you can become the best soccer player in the world."

Mia doesn't boast and didn't know how good she was until she made the national team.  "I knew I was better at soccer than at basketball, but I never really had a sense I was especially good," she said.

When she was 16, she dropped her other sports.  "That's when I decided soccer was the sport for me," she said.

**Mia in 1988, playing for the U.S. national women's soccer team.**

# *A World of Her Own*

$M$ia was very nervous as the U.S. played Sweden in the 1991 Women's World Cup. At 19, she was the team's youngest player, and she was having problems.

"The girl I was marking took me to school," Mia said. "I just didn't want to make a mistake." Mia made many mistakes in the game, but she scored the game-winning goal. She also scored a goal in the next game, and the U.S. won the title.

"When Mia is playing her best, there's no one better in the world," said Tony DiCicco, who became coach of the women's team in 1994.

Off the field, Mia is quiet. But on the soccer field she's determined and tough. "Mia's a little shy," DiCicco said. "But, she's not shy when she's faced up one-on-one in the front third of the field."

Mia played soccer in college for Anson Dorrance, the coach who scouted her for the national team. She led North Carolina to four NCAA titles, taking one year off to compete for the World Cup with the national team.

"Mia has this amazing ability to go right through defenders," Dorrance said. "The statistics prove it. But they won't show you her acceleration and grace. For that, you've got to watch her play."

The Tar Heels had a 92-1-2 record during Mia's career, losing only to the University of Connecticut. "She established standards in college for others to meet," said Dave Simeone, a former member of the U.S. coaching staff.

Mia graduated with a degree in political science in 1994. That December she married Christian Corry, a Marine Corps helicopter pilot.

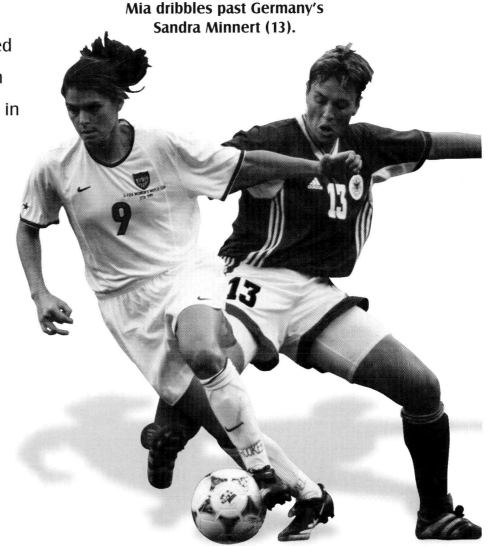

**Mia dribbles past Germany's Sandra Minnert (13).**

# Heart of Gold

When Mia was a senior in college, she got a phone call that filled her with excitement: she learned women's soccer would be a full-medal sport at the 1996 Olympics. "What an incredible opportunity," Mia said. "You hear all the clichés, that it's a dream come true. Well, it is for myself and for every girl growing up who plays any sport."

Mia had grown up idolizing Olympic stars such as Mary Lou Retton and Jackie Joyner-Kersee. Now she could be a role model for others. "This is incredible for me," Mia said.

The biggest crowd ever to see a women's sporting event watched the U.S. play the gold-medal game. Mia had sprained her ankle in a first-round game against Sweden, but was still able to score an overtime goal against Norway to put the Americans in the final against China.

In Athens, Georgia, the University of Georgia's Stanford Stadium was jam-packed. Flashbulbs sparkled and fired-up fans clapped their hands and stomped their feet. In the midst of all the noise and excitement, Mia ran down the field. She took a pass from Kristine Lilly near the goal and banged it with her left foot. The ball found teammate Shannon MacMillan, who booted it past China's goalkeeper, Gao Hong.

Later in the game, Mia broke past the person guarding her deep in the right corner and stopped. She passed to Joy Fawcett, who dribbled the ball and saw Tiffeny Milbrett running on the left side. She got it to Tiffeny, who scored.

Toward the end of the game, Mia was injured and left the field on a stretcher. After the United States won 2-1, she was carried onto the field for the victory celebration. "She works her heart out," Lilly said. "It's all about heart."

**Mia (right) and her German opponent go after the ball.**

# Triumph to Tragedy

Shortly after the thrill and joy of the Olympics, Mia experienced tragedy and pain. Her older brother Garrett died at age 28 from complications due to a rare blood disorder. Mia created a foundation to raise money for awareness of bone marrow disease and research. "No matter where I play, I feel Garrett is there," Mia said.

Her most satisfying moment off the soccer field came when bone marrow donors and recipients came together for the first time during halftime of an all-star exhibition game. The Mia Hamm Foundation also supports another cause important to Mia: helping girls play sports.

"I would not have had the life experiences to date without other pioneers who worked tirelessly to provide opportunities for women in sports," Mia said on her foundation's Web site. "I am committed to continue the progress made in the last decade."

Mia is happy that women's sports are becoming more popular, but she doesn't understand why so much attention is being focused on her. "It's weird getting attention. When companies want me to represent them, I think, 'Why me?'" she said.

Mia doesn't like being in the spotlight, but she does interviews and tolerates the attention to help make soccer more popular.

She credits soccer with helping her become strong and confident, and wants to pass that on to other girls.

"I am a shy person who will never be completely comfortable with all the attention," she said. "If it helps get our team out there, I'll do it. It's not for me, not for personal gain. I don't look at it as celebrity status. I want to do as much as I can to get the sport out there."

Soccer has helped Mia break out of her shell and express herself. "There is never a time you feel you are by yourself or alone," she said. "It's a powerful feeling of camaraderie."

It's no surprise that Mia compares life's ups and downs to a soccer game. "You get out of it exactly what you put into it," Mia said. "It can teach you so much. It's also humbling. You think you're doing great, then all of a sudden something happens. How do you go on from there? Same as soccer. You can out-shoot a team 20 to 2 and lose 1 to 0."

**Mia signs autographs for young fans.**

# A New Goal Standard

Mia's soccer success continued after the Olympics. She won her fifth consecutive U.S. Soccer Female Athlete of the Year award in 1998 and had a career-high 20 goals and 20 assists. She was the third player to score at least 100 international goals.

"That's unbelievable," Coach Dave Simeone said. "She's not finished anytime soon." She had three goals in a 5-0 win over Denmark that put the U.S. in the 1998 Goodwill Games final. The U.S. beat China to win the gold medal.

"It is really a team," Danish coach Jorgen Hvidemose said. "They function well together, and together they get chances for Mia."

The national team prepared for the 1999 World Cup with a series of exhibition games around the country. The U.S. had taken the bronze medal in the 1995 World Cup, but Mia didn't feel pressured to bring home the gold this time.

"The only pressure we have is to win the Cup because we want to," she said. In the months leading up to the Cup, Mia went through an eight-game scoring drought. But she didn't get discouraged.

"The higher you get, the harder it gets," Mia said. "People expect you to do it every night. Don't you think even Michael Jordan struggled at times? You can bet he did."

She didn't worry, and was happy to see her teammates do the scoring. "When Mia had that stretch without scoring goals, other players stepped up and got it done," DiCicco said.

When the Cup roster was unveiled in May, Mia had six goals and a team-high nine assists. "Goals help your confidence, and as a forward you feel that scoring is one of your jobs," she said. "But I want to do whatever I can to help our team win. If that means working hard defensively and not getting a shot on goal, then that's fine with me."

**Mia gets tripped up going for the ball.**

Mia soon broke out of her scoring drought, and was on her way to breaking the international goal-scoring record for men or women. On May 22, 1999, she took a pass from teammate Cindy Parlow and booted it past a Brazilian goalie to score her 108th goal, breaking the record that had been held by Elisabetta Vignotto of Italy. Mia had more international goals than even the legendary Pelé, who scored 77 in his career.

"That's huge," Simeone said. "But Mia would say it's an accomplishment and heap praise on those around her."

"She is the world's best," DiCicco said. "Who can argue with that right now?"

"When I was playing, they said soccer was a man's world and that women should remain on the sidelines," Pelé said. "All I can say is I'm glad I never had to go up against Mia Hamm."

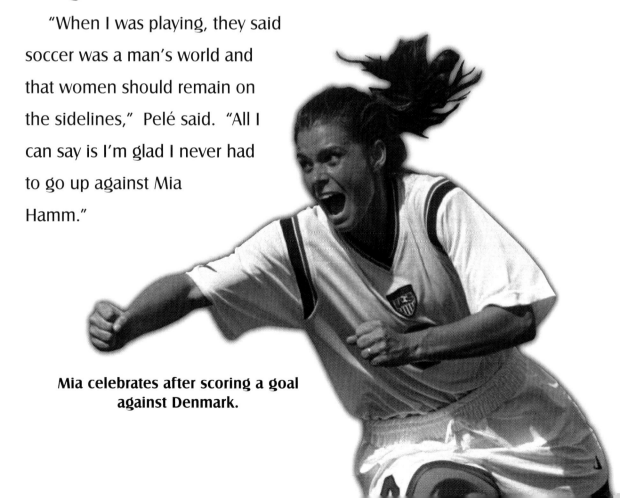

**Mia celebrates after scoring a goal against Denmark.**

# A World-Class Win

The United States was into soccer like never before during the 1999 Women's World Cup. The U.S. was favored to take the gold. "I think we're doing what we can to build the excitement," Mia said. "We can win. That's what every team wants to do. You don't play in the World Cup to do anything other than win. In that regard we're no different than any other team."

Everyone expected Mia to make it an exciting tournament. "When Mia touches the ball, you just feel great things are going to happen," U.S. co-captain Carla Overbeck said. "She has that Michael Jordan impact," Coach Dorrance said. "You might get to see something you've never seen before."

Mia, however, downplayed her ability. "I'm no better than a lot of people on this U.S. team," Mia said. "I learn that every day when I go against Kate Sobrero in practice. She doesn't care how many goals I've scored or what's written about me."

The United States beat Denmark, Nigeria, North Korea, Germany, and Brazil on its way to the gold-medal game with China. Mia was named to the World Cup All-Star team. "That's awesome," Mia said. "With all the great players, that's a real honor."

The U.S. knew China would be tough. China had broken the Americans' 50-game home winning streak, 2-1 in April. "It made us go back and refocus," Mia said of the loss. "We understand why we lost, and you try to go back and fix those things. You don't make those mistakes again."

The tournament was already a success in Mia's eyes. "This team has been able to bring about a lot of excitement and recognition for women's sports," she said. "People also realize how well other teams play and how entertaining our game is. The World Cup has achieved what all of us wanted it to."

A throng of fans yelling the names of their favorite players greeted the team's bus as it pulled into the Rose Bowl parking lot for the July 10 final. When the team took the field, the stadium in Pasadena, California, was packed with more than 90,000 fans. Many girls and boys wore Mia's No. 9 jersey.

**Mia poses with some of her teammates. From left: Kate Sobrero, Danielle Fotopoulos, Sara Whalen, Mia Hamm, Julie Foudy, Christie Pearce, and Brandi Chastain.**

A special fan was watching the game from President Bill Clinton's private box. Mia's husband Christian, who was stationed in Japan, had been given permission to return to see the game.

The gold-medal game was very close. China had a chance to score early in the first half, but Mia blocked Pu Wei's shot. After 90 minutes of tension-filled play in the searing heat, the game was tied 0-0. The women then played 30 minutes of overtime, with no score. The title would be decided by a shootout.

The U.S. and China both had made three penalty kicks when it was Mia's turn. She calmly faced Gao Hong and aimed toward the left side of the net. Boom! The ball rocketed past the goalie.

"I wanted to put it in a position she couldn't get," Mia said.

"All I saw was a ball in the back of the net. I don't even know if it was a good kick."

Moments later, when Chastain's final penalty kick went in the net, the Americans were world champions. The U.S. made all five of its penalty kicks, while China was four of five. The crowd wept with joy. Mia cheered and hugged her teammates. She had done what she had set out to do. Soccer was more popular than ever.

"I hope every young kid left the stadium today saying, 'I want to be there,'" Mia said.

# Mia Hamm Profile

Name: Mariel Margaret Hamm

Nickname: Mia

Birthdate: March 17, 1972

Birthplace: Selma, Alabama

Family: Christian Corry, husband;
Bill, Dad; Stephanie, Mom; two
sisters, three brothers (brother
Garrett died in 1996)

Height: 5-foot-5

Weight: 125 pounds

Hometown: Chapel Hill, North
Carolina

High School: Graduated from Lake Braddock Secondary School in
Burke, Virginia. Also attended Notre Dame High School in Wichita
Falls, Texas.

College: University of North Carolina

Position: Forward

# *Personal*

Was named one of the world's 50 most beautiful people by *People* magazine in 1997 ... Likes watching college basketball ... also plays golf and basketball ... played golf with basketball legend Michael Jordan, who also attended the University of North Carolina ... favorite color is green ... prefers Italian food ... has to tie her right shoe and then her left shoe before games ... role models are Chris Evert, Wayne Gretzky, Jackie Joyner-Kersee, and Michael Jordan for "the way they carried themselves on and off their respective fields of play."

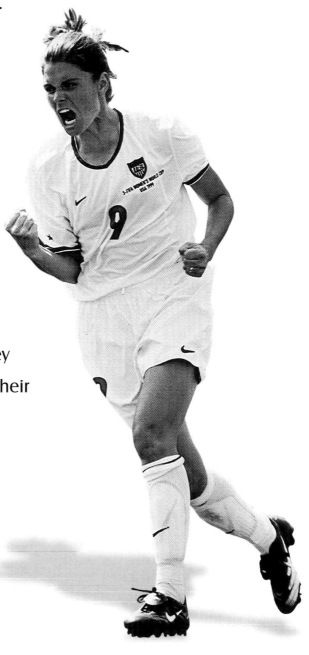

**Mia reacts after making a goal during the shootout of the gold-medal game of the World Cup.**

# *Chronology*

**March 17, 1972** - Mia Hamm is born in Selma, Alabama.

**August 3, 1987** - Makes first appearance for U.S. national team, vs. China. At age 15, she is the youngest female ever to play for the U.S.

**1989** - Graduates from Lake Braddock Secondary School in Burke, Virginia.  Begins college at the University of North Carolina, winning first of four national titles with the Tar Heels.

**July 25, 1990** - Scores first goal for U.S. national team, vs. Norway.

**1991** - At age 19, she is the youngest member of the World-Cup winning U.S. national team. Starts five of USA's six World-Cup games in China, scoring two goals.

**1992** - Wins Hermann Award as best female player in college soccer.

**1993** - Wins Hermann Award again.

**May, 1994** - Graduates from the University of North Carolina with a degree in political science.

**1995** - Has 19 goals and 18 assists for 56 points as U.S. national team goes 17-2-2. Plays several minutes at goalkeeper against Denmark in the World Cup when regular goalie Briana Scurry was ejected and the U.S. had used all of its substitutes.

**1996** - Member of Olympic champion U.S. national team. Sets up both U.S. goals in the title match.

**1997** - Scores 18 goals as U.S. national team goes 14-2-0. Named by *People* magazine as one of the world's 50 most beautiful people.

**1998** - Sets career-highs in goals (20), assists (20) and points (60) as U.S. team goes 18-1-2. Leads U.S. to the first Goodwill Games gold medal for women's soccer. Scores five of the team's seven goals, including both in a win over China in the final. Wins ESPY Award for Outstanding Female Athlete.

**1999** - Named to the Women's World Cup All-Star team. Makes penalty kick to help U.S. win gold-medal game over China.

**1999** - Named Sportswomen of the Year by the Women's Sports Foundation.

**Mia after being awarded the MVP of the 1997 Women's Cup.**

# *Awards and Honors*

High school All-America

All-time leading scorer in Atlantic Coast Conference women's soccer, with 103 goals and 72 assists

All-time leading scorer in NCAA soccer tournament, with 16 goals and nine assists in 13 games

Hermann Award winner as best female player in college soccer (1992, 1993)

Won four NCAA championships with the University of North Carolina (1989, 1990, 1992, 1993)

Three-time college All-America

Won the NCAA's Honda Broderick Award for female college sports (1993-94)

Had her jersey retired by the University of North Carolina (1994)

Most Valuable Player of the Chiquita Cup (1994)

U.S. Soccer Female Athlete of the Year (1994, 1995, 1996, 1997, 1998)

MVP of U.S. Women's Cup (1995, 1997)

Member of U.S. women's national team that won a gold medal in the 1991 World Cup

Member of U.S. women's national team that won a gold medal at the 1996 Olympics

Named Women's Sports Foundation Athlete of the Year (1997)

Led U.S. to the first Goodwill Games gold medal (1998)

Scored five of the team's seven goals, including both goals in a win over China in the Goodwill Games championship

Won 1998 ESPY Award for Outstanding Female Athlete

Named to the Women's World Cup all-star team (1999)

Named Sportswomen of the Year (1999)

## Mia Hamm's Statistics with the U.S. National Team

| Year | GP/GS | MIN | G | A | W-L-T |
|---|---|---|---|---|---|
| 1987 | 7/4 | 369 | 0 | 0 | 4-2-1 |
| 1988 | 8/7 | 554 | 0 | 0 | 3-3-2 |
| 1989 | 1/0 | 40 | 0 | 0 | 0-0-1 |
| 1990 | 5/1 | 270 | 4 | 1 | 5-0-0 |
| 1991 | 28/24 | 1,820 | 10 | 4 | 21-6-1 |
| 1992 | 2/2 | 136 | 1 | 0 | 0-2-0 |
| 1993 | 16/16 | 1,304 | 10 | 4 | 12-4-0 |
| 1994 | 9/9 | 810 | 10 | 5 | 8-1-0 |
| 1995 | 21/20 | 1,790 | 19 | 18 | 17-2-2 |
| 1996 | 23/23 | 1,777 | 9 | 18 | 21-1-1 |
| 1997 | 16/16 | 1,253 | 18 | 6 | 14-2-0 |
| 1998 | 21/21 | 1,576 | 20 | 20 | 18-1-2 |
| **Totals:** | **157/143** | **11,699** | **101** | **76** | **123-24-10** |

KEY: GP - Games played; GS - Games started; MIN - Minutes played; G - Goals; A - Assists; W-L-T - Record in games Hamm played in.

# Glossary

**ATHLETICISM** - The vigorous, active qualities found in people who do well in sports.

**AWE** - An emotion that combines respect, fear, and wonder.

**CONFIDENCE** - Feeling you have the power to succeed.

**FORWARD** - Offensive position on a soccer team. Her main job is to score goals.

**FOUNDATION** - An organization that supports a cause for a long period of time.

**GOAL** - A point. Also, the area the ball must enter for a point to be scored.

**INTERNATIONAL PLAY** - Competition between teams from different countries.

**MVP** - Most Valuable Player.

**OLYMPICS** - Contests between athletes from many countries. The Olympics include summer and winter games.

**PENALTY KICK (PK)** - A free kick at the goal made from a point 12 yards out in front of the goal. It is allowed for certain violations within a designated area around the goal. Penalty kicks are also used to decide the outcome of a game tied after overtime.

**RESPONSIBILITY** - To be accountable for something.

**SHOOTOUT** - A means of deciding the outcome of a game tied after overtime, in which each team tries five penalty kicks.

**TITLE** - A championship.

**TOURNAMENT** - Series of games.

**WORLD CUP** - Series of soccer games held every four years to determine the world champion. It is soccer's most important tournament. There are men's and women's tournaments.

To make a donation to the Mia Hamm Foundation, contact:

Mia Hamm Foundation

1 Hampshire Court

Durham, North Carolina, 27713

or visit the Web site: www.miafoundation.org

# *Index*